ideals® CHRISTMAS

May these be your gifts
   at Christmas:
Warm hearts and shining faces
Surrounding you to make your home
The happiest of places.

May these be your gifts at Christmas:
Deep peace and lasting love
That you will share together
With the ones you're fondest of.

—AUTHOR UNKNOWN

IDEALS PUBLICATIONS

NASHVILLE, TENNESSEE

Time for Christmas

Fred Bauer

Christmas is a time of anticipation,
When hope becomes a shining star,
When children's wishes become prayers,
And days are X'ed on the calendar.

Christmas is a time for healing,
When disagreers and disagreements meet,
When long-time wounds are mended
And love moves hatred to retreat.

Christmas is a time for patience,
When we try anew to mold
Our lives in the image of Him
Whose birthday we uphold.

Christmas is a time for giving,
The Wise Men brought their best,
But Christ showed that the gift of self
Will out-give all the rest.

Christmas is a time for understanding
People and customs throughout the world,
When for all-too-brief a season,
The banner of peace is unfurled.

Christmas is a time for children
No matter what their age,
Spirit is the only ticket,
And heart is the only gauge.

Christmas is a time for learning,
A time when new truths unfold,
And not-so-innocent children
Often teach the old.

Christmas is a time for sharing,
A time for needy hands to clasp,
A time for stretching out in faith
With a reach that exceeds our grasp.

Christmas is a time for love,
A time for inhibitions to shed,
A time for showing that we care,
A time for words too long unsaid.

Christmas is a time to remember
Timeless stories from days of yore,
A time to ponder what's ahead,
A time to open another door.

A Christmas Letter

Nancy Esher

I have tried in vain to think of a Christmas gift I could send to all of you. Instead, I send you a wish. I wish for you a special Christmas tree. I hope it will be a tall and straight tree with boughs outstretched to shelter you this coming year. Trim it with love; surround it with faith.

This Christmas tree will have a bright and shining star at the very top. It will shine through the darkness around you and bring hope to the world as it did so many years ago in Bethlehem. May its radiance flood your heart in the days ahead.

Under this tree there shall be presents for each of you. One is a package filled with memories. These are not ordinary memories. These are of special people, of special times, and of other Christmas seasons from the past.

There is another package under this tree for you. It is filled with peace. Share it with the world. To settle for less is to make mockery of the words, "Peace on earth, goodwill toward men." And indeed, peace is the foundation upon which the tree I wish for you shall stand.

I hope that this tree will be a part of all the good times that will be yours this season, helping to make this Christmas the merriest of all.

And I wish each of you a very happy Christmas Day.

Christmas Shoppers

Aileen Fisher

Oh, the wind is brisk and biting
and the cold is not inviting,
but there's music, merry music, everywhere.
The streets are full of bustle
and our feet are full of hustle,
for there's Christmas, merry Christmas in the air.

Oh, the wind is cold and chilly
and it whistles at us shrilly,
but there's music, merry music, everywhere.
The bells are full of ringing
and our hearts are full of singing,
for there's Christmas, merry Christmas, in the air.

Light of the Season

Elizabeth A. Hobsek

Passing by the shops in town
Such wonders there I see:
A holly pin with berries bright
Gleaming back at me.
At Center Square, where
    four lanes cross,
Stands a decorated tree.

Potted red poinsettia plants
Arrayed in foiled row
Catch glints of winter sunshine
To make their Yuletide show.
And every balsam wreath's
    displayed
With a sparkling crimson bow.

Figures lit near Manger scene
From a church nearby,
Surround the Child's
    straw-filled crib,
Greeting passersby.
Traffic signals, red and green,
Blink against the sky.

Our joyful hearts fill with cheer;
For home and hearth each pines.
Everything that glistens here,
Every lamp that shines
Reminds us Christmas Day
    is near—
Resplendent are the signs!

CHRISTMAS SLEIGH PARADE by Ann Stookey. Image © 2011 Ann Stookey/Applejack Art Partners

THROUGH MY WINDOW

READ ALL ABOUT IT

Pamela Kennedy

*I*t's time to get going on the annual Christmas newsletter again. For a long time I resisted writing one of these missives. I believed that the only *good* way to write a Christmas letter was by hand. But a few years ago, after suffering a bout of near-paralyzing writer's cramp, I decided to dip my toe into the wide water of Christmas newsletter composition. I vowed, however, not to write one of *those* newsletters. You know the ones I'm talking about: extremely long, single-spaced, and written in a font only a gnat could read. And I certainly wasn't going to brag about my kids accomplishing feats of valor or earning PhDs in some obscure field of science. (Of course, it helped that none of my offspring had actually done any of these things. But if they ever did, I wouldn't brag about it in a Christmas newsletter.) No, my newsletter would be short, to the point, interesting, creative, but not too cutesy. It would not, for example, be written by the cat.

Having thus defined my task, I decided to aim for a half-sheet of paper that I could tuck into a traditional Christmas card. But after typing up half a page about our family, I thought it looked boring. So I changed the font color to red. That looked too much like the emergency instructions on our smoke alarm. So I changed the font color

to green. *Hmmm.* One long paragraph didn't look very interesting, even in green. Then I recalled that one of my students had written a paragraph about herself and somehow shaped the sentences into a profile of a woman's head. I thought I might be able to pull off a seasonal shape of some sort. A star was too complicated, and I couldn't figure out how to do a candle or a wreath. Then I had it! A Christmas tree! I hit the centering button on my word processing program and then just started out with one word. Then the next line had two, and so on until I had created a triangular shaped piece of writing with a few short lines at the bottom of the triangle to resemble the tree's trunk. It looked pretty cool, if I do say so myself. Brimming with Christmas spirit, I decided to jazz it up a bit by making alternating lines red and green. There wasn't much news in it, due to the design, but it certainly fit the criteria of being short and unique.

The next year I decided to try out one of those online templates where you just fill in the blanks and replace the pictures of the happy computer family with your own photos. How hard could that be? I discovered there were dozens of templates from which to choose. Unfortunately, many of them required a level of computer expertise beyond my own. Finally I found one with directions I understood that didn't ask me to purchase services I'd never use. After puttering around for an hour or two, I created quite a lovely page and hit the print button. What I hadn't realized was that this particular template consisted of seven more pages! Really? Does anyone ever write, let alone read, an eight-page Christmas newsletter? Well, I got around that by just printing off the first page. Even my kids were impressed that year (well, except for my oldest, who took umbrage with the euphemism I used to describe his lengthy period of unemployment).

So now what do I do this year, for an encore? I just finished checking out websites with information for Christmas newsletter authors like me. What I found most fascinating were the optional add-ons to "make your newsletter stand out from the rest!" Apparently, you can create your own postage stamps by using a program operated by the US Postal Service. And then, if you really want to go overboard, you can address and stamp all your newsletters and mail them in a big envelope to some place in Anchorage, Alaska, that will send them off with a "North Pole" postmark. If you want something less predictable, there are places in Bethlehem, Pennsylvania, or Santa Claus, Indiana, that will do the same thing. Honestly, who looks at the postmarks on their envelopes? If the holiday postmark is a bit too much, how about return address labels or stickers with portraits of your family or pets dressed up in holiday

attire? There appears to be no end to all the ways one might personalize the Christmas newsletter. I found a site for intellectuals (or maybe just people who want to irritate their friends and family) that allows you to create your Christmas letter as a multiple choice quiz or a crossword puzzle. What's a six-letter word for where we took our summer vacation? I'm not sure anyone on my Christmas card list has the time to sit down with a pencil and figure out what I've been up to all year.

So maybe I'll just go with a simple letter this Christmas, printed on some of that decorated computer paper you can buy at the drugstore. For a change, I'll type it up in black. But perhaps I'll use a slightly larger font this year—my friends and family aren't getting any younger!

CHRISTMAS TREES REMEMBERED

Bob Artley

From my earliest years, the Christmas tree was a part of my accumulated impressions, which have built up since then into a rich store of Christmas memories.

One of the very first Christmas trees I remember came from a tall spruce in our front yard. Dad had already decided it would be cut down because the yard was so dense and shaded with evergreens that grass would not grow under them. So it was decided that the spruce's removal would begin by cutting off its top for our Christmas tree.

A day or two before Christmas, while Mom and I watched from an upstairs bedroom window, Dad climbed to the top of the tall spruce near our front porch. He secured a rope around the portion that was to be our Christmas tree, then sawed it off and gently lowered it to the snowy yard below.

When that little tree, which only moments before had been living up somewhere near heaven, stood green and fresh in our living room, waiting to be adorned, it all seemed a part of the Christmas magic. The boughs were wet from melted snow and were cold and prickly to the touch. The magic fragrance of fresh evergreen that is so much a part of Christmas flooded the room.

Once we had exhausted the supply of fresh trees from our front yard, we made our selection from the bedraggled collection of little trees that leaned against the outside wall of the local grocery store.

I can still see my parents choosing the tree. Dad would reach in among the branches of one of the trees, grasp it around its trunk, raise it up, and bring it down sharply, thumping its sawed butt against the frozen ground or cement sidewalk. If this "shock test" didn't jolt its needles loose, it was a likely candidate to stand in front of the west window of our farmhouse living room for a few days to help us celebrate Christmas.

Selecting the right tree was not easy. But it was remarkable how, from that forlorn stock of compressed and misshapen tree specimens, there could be chosen one that, when set up and decorated and put in a place of honor in the home, would be transformed into a thing of beauty and meaning.

Our family Christmas tree was usually put up and lovingly decorated for the great celebration only a day or two before Christmas. This short period of display not only assured the physical freshness of the tree but also the freshness of its presence in the room.

In the days before electricity on the farm, we could not use colored tree lights. But our Christmas tree, with its tinsel and its foil-covered stars reflecting the warm light of the kerosene lamps in the room, shone and sparkled much like the moon and other cold heavenly bodies reflect the light of the sun. I thought it was every bit as beautiful a Christmas tree as those adorned with electric lights.

So, whether or not the tree was "perfect" didn't matter to those gathered around it, as long as it was a fresh evergreen with the special fragrance that meant Christmas. In spite of any imperfections, our family Christmas tree became the center of our merry gathering of fun and goodwill.

Bits & Pieces

Our house is open, Lord, to thee;
Come in, and share our Christmas tree!
We've made each nook and corner bright,
Burnished with yellow candlelight.
—*Luci Shaw*

One of the sweetest sights of all is a child
in pajamas, peeking wide-eyed around the
corner at the Christmas tree and all the
brightly wrapped gifts underneath.
—*Author Unknown*

The tree is full of trimmings
And gifts for girl and boy.
The world is full of Christmas cheer;
Our hearts are full of joy.
—*Author Unknown*

Likely the reason we all go so haywire at Christmastime, with endless unrestrained and often silly buying of gifts, is that we don't quite know how to put our love into words.

—Harlan Miller

Happy, happy Christmas, that can win us back to the delusions of our childhood days, recall to the old man the pleasures of his youth, and transport the traveler back to his own fireside and quiet home!

—Charles Dickens

The best of all gifts around any Christmas tree is the presence of a happy family all wrapped up in each other.

—Burton Hills

It is good to be children sometimes, and never better than at Christmas, when its mighty Founder was a child Himself.

—Charles Dickens

CHRISTMAS JOY

Emmy Arnold

Oh, to become like a child again! Perhaps my beautiful childhood Christmas experiences spring from the fact that I was born on Christmas Day. Or perhaps it is simply that no one can feel the joy of Christmas quite like a child can.

Each year, a hundred days before Christmas, we children would begin to count down the days: *Only a hundred times more I will wake up in the morning, and then, hurrah! It's Christmas Day!* And, when at six o'clock on the eve of the First Sunday of Advent the bells rang in the Advent season, it seemed as though the angels were exulting; and we little children joined in; "O welcome, thou blessed Christmastime!" From that day on, the joy and eagerness for what was to come mounted with each day. Sometimes in the evening, when I was looking out into the darkness of the still night, I would think I saw God's angels coming down to proclaim the Christmas message to us. The breath of Christmas peace blew down like a greeting from heaven; all the sounds around us turned into Christmas music: "Lift up your heads, ye mighty gates; / Behold, the Lord of glory comes!"

Although the celebration of Christmas has been exploited for commercial reasons and the meaning of the season is often lost, we all feel the impulse at this time of year to think of others, to show love to others, to be there for others. It is a

Photograph © Belinda Images/SuperStock

feeling of human solidarity, the exulting of joy in one another, the certainty of mutual love. The brightness and fragrance of the living Christmas tree under which gifts are laid—here is light and warmth, symbolizing life and love.

A child, thinking of these Christmas symbols and gifts, might ask himself, *Can this be an excitement that soon will fade away?* No, is the answer, for all this is not yet the best and the best cannot pass. "God so loved the world that He gave His only Son." Of all gifts there is none so precious as this one. Therefore we ask only for this one gift: Stay with us, Lord Jesus Christ!

When as a child I stood before the lighted crib scene, I often fell into a deep reverie. I saw the Christ Child in His eternal light; I felt the same awe that the shepherds felt when they came to the crib to worship the little Child. It was there that I first realized what the joy of worship means. God's greatness came in the smallness of the Child in the crib.

> When in awe my heart is still
> and tries to grasp this miracle,
> all I can do is pray to God
> and feel how endless is His love.
>
> God became man for our own sake;
> God's Child, with us in flesh united.
> How could God hate us when He gives
> us what He, past all measure, loves?
>
> Love Him who with love is burning,
> see the star who on us pours
> light and comfort!

Anyone who as a child has looked into God's loving heart can never despair of his life, however hard it may be.

Joy radiates peace. Love brings peace. "I proclaim to you great joy that shall come to all peoples—peace on earth!" The true Christmas experience is to feel that this Christmas peace is the greater power; that even now, on earth, it overcomes all discord. That this peace shall come to all—that is the expectation and the faith of Christmas!

The Christmas star in the night sky, the shining of the Christmas light in the night—all this is the sign that light breaks into the darkness. Though we see about us the darkness, the light shall shine and drive it out. "The people who walked in darkness have seen a great light; those who dwelt in a land of deep darkness, on them has light shined."

Jesus is the light. Nobody else is the light; others can only witness to the light.

> The eternal light shall come to earth
> and give it a new radiance;
> it shines into the midst of night
> and makes us children of the light.

Only those who are reborn as children shall become children of the light. Wherever the Christmas Child is born in a heart, wherever Jesus begins His earthly life anew—that is where the life of God's love and of God's peace dawns again.

The Story of Christmas

Eileen Spinelli

How familiar—
the bright star that
beckoned kings from
their tinseled revelries . . .
the shepherds trodding
hill and stream
with lowing sheep . . .
angels winging,
singing above an old barn . . .
Joseph lighting a lantern . . .
Mary tucking a blanket . . .
a baby's soft breath.
How familiar the story
told bedside,
fireside,
curbside in the snow:
no room at the inn.
We know it well enough.
And yet
when there seems to be
no newness in it at all,
we are called,
snagged,
dragged from our merry rooms,
our nests and our tents.
Listen! Is it the wind
or winter bird
or simply grace
that adds the shining word
of wonderment?

Our Treasured Traditions

GRAMMY'S CRÈCHE

Elaine St. Johns

My mother, known as "Grammy" to her grandchildren, started the tradition after I moved to California with my two-year-old daughter, Kristen, and six-year-old son, George. We all lived together, along with an aunt and uncle and various friends and relations, on a family property we called "The Hill."

Grammy had decided that more than one Christmas tree was redundant, so that year, she instead bought for her house a sturdy, rustic, peak-roofed shed; charming Mary and Joseph figurines; a small wooden manger; and, of course, the Royal Infant Himself. She set them all up on a living room table surrounded with holiday greens and poinsettias. (The Infant was kept hidden snugly out of sight until Christmas Eve.) The children thought the merry Christmas tree at our house was for "pretty"; but the crèche at Grammy's house, where we gathered on Christmas Eve (when Baby Jesus magically appeared), was the focus of reverence and awe.

Kristen and George, enchanted by the crèche, started to save their pocket money to add to Grammy's set. On those long-ago Christmas Eves, as we read the Christmas story from the Gospels, the children would present their gifts. One year, an exotic Wise Man; another, four tiny shepherds and one too-large sheep; then a blue

ceramic donkey and a plump porcelain angel with a rose atop her head.

All too soon, the children grew up, married, and moved away. And Grammy's work as a writer led her to move permanently to a hotel in New York. The Hill was no more and the crèche went into storage.

Then my granddaughter, Jessica, was born. Just before Jessica's first Christmas, a large package was delivered to me from the storage warehouse. The card read, "From one grandmother to another." It was Grammy's crèche. And there they were—Mary and Joseph and Jesus, the Wise Man, the big sheep and too-small shepherds, the blue donkey minus one ear, the angel sans rose—but what matter? I carefully set the scene on a table in the living room. After all, more than one Christmas tree is redundant!

Before this manger scene, Jessica and later her brother, Bogart, learned the blessed Christmas story and beloved carols. And then they began to bring gifts to the stable. An early offering was a tiny gift-wrapped package of peanuts. Later, with allowances hoarded throughout December, Christmas by Christmas, arrived a variety of angels, several deer, a cow, and more odd sheep. Although not every beast of the field or monster of the sea gathered before the Holy Family, there did appear a

white horse, an otter, a lion, a handsome orang-utan, Jonah's whale, and, since Bo found out what behemoth meant, a hippopotamus.

Grammy's crèche became a neighborhood attraction, with all the children dropping by each year during Christmas week to watch it grow.

Two years ago, Jessica and Bo made an Advent wreath to place at the manger site, and each of the four Sundays before Christmas we ceremoniously lighted a candle and sang carols. This past year they arranged the scene themselves, using my brick fireplace with its raised hearth. Books were stacked to form a series of gentle terraces to the hearth and were covered with a white sheet and cotton snow. The fireplace was filled with pine boughs from the yard, and on the hearth itself sat the crèche with its familiar, well-loved figures.

On Christmas Eve, as Jessica, now ten, placed the Infant in His manger and her mother, father, Bo, and I sang one last "Silent Night," I inwardly thanked my mother for her gift. Not only for the tangible objects themselves but also for her gift of wisdom in establishing a tradition that strengthens our family and its sense of continuity. For one day, in the not-too-distant future, I will give my daughter Grammy's crèche with a note: "From one grandmother to another."

Giving
James E. Feig

May all your gifts at Christmas be
Bright packages beneath your tree,
Filled with blessings from above
And cheerful smiles from those you love;
Filled with happiness untold,
Lasting friendships, new and old;
Peace and joy, contentment too,
Enough to last the whole year through.

My Love
Georgia B. Adams

Somehow I wish I could wrap up,
In package bright and gay,
All of the love I have for you
This joyous Christmas Day!

I'd find the largest box I could
And pack it in real tight;
Oh, I would do most anything
To make your season bright!

And so the purpose I've in mind
Is just to let you know
That every thought I have of you
Just seems to grow and grow.

And though my love can't be contained
In package large and gay,
I'm sure you know it deeper grows
With every Christmas Day!

THE SECRET OF HAPPY GIVING

Catherine Marshall

Christmas—the time for giving and receiving gifts—is here again. Nowadays the store decorations go up before Thanksgiving is over. Pondering the commercialism that seems to characterize this holiday season, I began to wonder if the Bible had anything to say about gifts and giving that might be helpful.

When I turned to it, one portion of the Sermon on the Mount seemed especially pertinent. If we stand in the temple, Jesus said (Matthew 5:23–24), about to offer a gift to God, and suddenly remember that a friend has a grudge or resentment against us, we are to postpone giving the gift. We are to go and be reconciled to our friend, then come back and offer our gift to God; only then will He receive our offering and bless us. Relationships are primary, He seems to be saying; gifts secondary.

Does this command apply to all gift-giving, I wondered, or only to those gifts labeled expressly for God? With this question in mind, I turned to other Scripture passages. I was amazed to see, first, how frequently the giving of gifts is mentioned in the Bible. And second, how in every case the gift springs out of and is symbolic of a relationship, good or bad. Rebekah accepts gifts of jewelry and clothing, symbolic of her acceptance of Isaac as her husband. Jacob tries to give a lavish present of livestock to the brother he has wronged, but Esau refuses. Later on, Jacob singles out one of his sons for the gift of a beautiful coat, demonstrating his favoritism and fostering jealousy among the brothers. Wise men bring gifts to an Infant—gold which acknowledges their King, frankincense their God, myrrh their Redeemer.

It should not surprise us that the person-to-person dimension is important. The Kingdom of God is the kingdom of right relationships. That's what matters to Him.

When the relationship is right, how precious the gift becomes. I remember the autumn my father spent many weeks making my Christmas gift—a doll bed, dresser, and china cupboard. To this day I can shut my eyes and see that miniature furniture, painted white with glass knobs on the drawers and cupboard doors. But surely the reason I remember it so fondly and in such detail is that the gift spoke of the father-daughter relationship behind it. The handmade furniture said, "I love you; you are important to me—important enough to be worth any amount of my time and my very best effort."

Such gifts are a spontaneous expression of unselfish love. But can we say the same for all the gifts that we give at Christmastime? Isn't it true that sometimes we use the device of a gift to conceal or paper over a flawed relationship? Or—even more common— isn't our attitude sometimes: "I'm giving you this gift because I feel I must (because you expect it, or because you're likely to give me something and I must reciprocate, or because I don't know how to get out of this bleak and joyless exchange)"?

Perhaps this Christmas all of us should examine our gift list to see if any of our giving falls into that category. If so, why not try the happy experiment of applying Jesus' priority to the situation: first be reconciled to your brother, then offer your gift.

We could try it with just one person. As we look down our list, is there anyone for whom we invariably have trouble finding a gift? Is there someone we resent shopping for? Anyone with whom we feel uncomfortable, no matter what we give them? Those can be clues to relationships that need mending.

Once we have selected the person, the next step is to devote time each day to thinking and praying about the relationship. Is the person a neighbor or a coworker? Perhaps we've never really focused on him as a human being. We have not cared enough even to seek out his needs and preferences.

The answer here could be a lunch date, a visit to his home, half an hour of real conversation. Does some old, never-acknowledged resentment lie between us and some member of the family? Healing could take the form of a letter, a face-to-face meeting, or simply an interior act of confession.

Whatever the relationship we choose to work on and whatever the steps we take to improve it, we should wait until we are satisfied that it is as close to the one God intended as we can make it. Only then should we proceed with the secondary matter of selecting a gift. The price tag will not matter, as our gift does what all true gifts do—it reflects transparent love.

When we give in that spirit, we are truly making ready for Christmas when Love itself comes down to earth. Then with the Wise Men, we too can kneel at His crib and give thanks for the greatest gift of all.

Let Us Go Back!

Frank H. Keith

Let us go back to the beauties
That are pocketed deep in our past—
The joys we relinquished with childhood
But that hauntingly linger and last!

Let us return to the Christmas
That remains with the children of time—
The Christmas of wonderful wishes,
Of stardust and snowdrift and chime!

Let us go back to the vision
Of evergreen peace in our rooms,
Gay ribbons on gifts of the giving,
And the dream that consistently blooms.

Let us in piety wander
Where the veil of the centuries parts
To look at a Crib and an Infant,
Then Christmas will live in our hearts!

This Would I Keep

Grace Noll Crowell

This would I keep forever in my heart
Among the things the ruthless years may leave:
The glad excitement, wonder, and delight
Of Christmas Eve.

This would I hold untarnished through the years,
Although the roads I take may lead me far:
The radiant molten glory of the light
From one white star.

And oh, to keep the breathlessness, the thrill,
The heart's swift running out to meet surprise,
Never to lose entirely the light
Of childhood from my eyes;

Never to lose the Christmas morning joy,
And never the quick bright eagerness to give—
God, someway let my spirit keep the shine
Of Christmas while I live.

Photograph © Jessie Walker

Candlelight Service

Nancy A. Brackett

The church lies dimly lit with candles;
A hush falls from the darkened sky.
On the face of every person
Is lit a star in every eye.

Quietly the Christmas message
Is read aloud for all to hear,
Filling the room, a gentle magic
Warms every heart and fills each ear.

In voices ever sweet and strong,
How lovely do the anthems ring,
Filling the night with Christmas carols;
Of peace on Earth, goodwill, they sing.

And just outside in heavenly splendor,
Surrounding the church and all below,
The footprints of a million angels
Rest, glistening on the fallen snow.

Touch the World

Louisa Godissart McQuillen

It's Christmas.
Winter's calling, snow is falling,
all the land lies robed in white.

It's Christmas.
Enter, Jesus, warm my spirit,
touch the world through me tonight!

PARENTS PRAY, CHILDREN PLAY *by Nicky Boehme.*
Image © 2011 Nicky Boehme/McGaw Graphics

CHRISTMAS EVE: A LITTLE LIGHT FOR THE NEW YEAR

Derek Maul

Today has to be my absolute favorite of all the special days. Christmas Eve is joy multiplied. It's a day loaded with the stardust, dreams, and deep magic of all our accumulated wonder.

It seems sometimes that the echo of all our childhood joys covers December 24. The goodwill possible in all people colors even the mundane gestures of common life. Don't you feel the tingling in the air? Isn't it true that even the honks of cars, the bark of neighborhood dogs, and the noises of business sound friendlier today?

I even enjoy Christmas Eve shopping, so I typically pick up a few small stocking-stuffer gifts at the last minute simply because I can't get enough of the festive atmosphere. I like the sense of immediacy, the urgency, the unapologetic Christmas high.

Every example of goodwill proclaims Christ's coming. Every genuine outbreak of "Christmas Spirit" speaks God's blessing. Every gracious act of love, gesture of peace, and inkling of hope proclaims the witness of the shepherds. Each resounding experience of joy cries out with passion the reality of God's creative and redeeming love. What a dark world this would be without Christ! What an empty festival of winter would remain if God had not so loved this world.

Most of us have something special we look forward to, some aspect of celebration that best sums up the whole ball of wax when it comes to Christmas joy. These are the moments of pure epiphany where all the celebration, all the hope, all the meaning, and all the excitement seem to be wrapped up in a single instant.

My moment often happens in church, usually about halfway through the candle-lighting on Christmas Eve. The sanctuary is completely dark, with the exception of the "Christ Candle," and I enjoy the privilege of standing with the choir, slightly elevated, playing "Silent Night" on my acoustic guitar. It's a moment I anticipate every year.

The minister takes the flame and lights several candles, each one held by a leader in the church. Then, spreading out through the congregation, the elders carry their lights to the end of each row. Hundreds of people, young and old, touch wick to wick with naked flame.

It is then, with the light still reproducing but not yet complete, that it comes to me afresh why I love Christmas so much. In a world under siege by those who would seek to condemn; on a planet where it is so much easier to say what we are against than what we are for; in a society where the loudest sound we hear is often cynicism, argument, and complaint; where the clamor of war at times can be overwhelming—there is a more excellent way; there is a path that strives to illuminate rather than to destroy. There is a light we can pass, a light by which we can brighten every human heart we choose to touch and bring healing to every place where God's grace directs us to serve.

Because of Christmas, we have received the gift of recognizing what happens when darkness is confronted by light. This particular evening, looking out over a multitude of people drawn from the shadows by the compelling light of the Gospel, I find myself thinking about the coming new year.

The faces of a family I know to be struggling are captured in the glow, and I pray God's peace. A lost teenager smiles into her candle, so I ask God to show her the way home. My mind wanders to the Middle East, and I notice four children moving their lips in prayer—their father is serving in Iraq. I realize how much stronger love is than fear and how powerful are its messengers once released—equipped—into the world.

For me such moments of insight also serve to set the stage perfectly for the coming new year, a time often associated with a kind of post-holiday letdown. Decorations come down; lights hang, unlit, well into the January grayness; hope is stuffed into cardboard boxes; and the joy that held Advent truth so eloquently too readily dissolves.

That is why I am so grateful that—once the candles are lit—my guitar playing is joined by hundreds of voices singing, ever so tenderly, "Son of God, love's pure light; radiant beams from Thy holy face, with the dawn of redeeming grace. . . ."

And the grace-filled congregation leaves the sanctuary, carrying a light that will never fade in the dreary January days that can so easily disappoint.

Christmas in the Woods

Frances Frost

Tonight when the hoarfrost falls on the wood,
And the rabbit cowers, and the squirrel is cold,
And the horned owl huddles against a star,
And the drifts are deep, and the year is old,
All shy creatures will think of Him.
The shivering mouse, the hare,
    the wild young fox,
The doe with the startled fawn
Will dream of gentleness and a Child:

The buck with budding horns will turn
His starry eyes to a silver hill tonight.
The chipmunk will awake and stir
And leave his burrow for the chill,
    dark midnight.
And all timid things will pause and sigh,
    and sighing, bless
That Child who loves the trembling hearts,
The shy hearts of the wilderness.

One Night

Marchette Chute

Last winter when the snow was deep
And sparkled on the lawn
And there was moonlight everywhere,
I saw a little fawn.

I watched her playing in the snow;
She did not want to leave.
She must have known before she came
That it was Christmas Eve.

A Very Special Christmas Gift

Anne Penrod

A friendly red-clad visitor came early Christmas morn
And chirped a song that seemed to say, "The King of kings is born!"
He sang his cheerful melody despite the bitter cold
And made me glad that he had come to serenade my soul.

I lay and listened peacefully to all he had to say
And even caught a glimpse of him before he flew away.
His striking scarlet plumage—oh-so-dark against the snow—
Reminded me of God's great gift, that Christmas long ago.

For Jesus Christ, the Word made flesh, was born that special night,
And God, through Him, would change our sins from scarlet-red to white.
No wonder God's creation lifts a thankful voice and sings
To celebrate the Savior and the gifts His presence brings.

And likewise, Christmas morning snow, so virgin-white and new,
Is Father God reminding us what only He can do.
And though the snow will melt away and bird-sung songs may cease,
The greatest gift of all remains—God's Son, the Prince of Peace.

Early Christmas Morning

Nanci Roth Natale

Early Christmas morning,
Church bells fill the silence of home,
Where children still sleep
In sugarplum-filled dreams.
The sky lightens at a slow pace:
Pale pink-orange at the horizon,
Changing ever so subtly,
Purple, gray, light blue, and finally
A pure white gray up near heaven—
A brilliant hope-filled light
Against bare winter trees and
    hard ground.

Still early, the trees shudder slightly
In the cold awakening of pre-dawn
Slowly lighting the earth,

Waking people everywhere.
Noisy children waken now,
Their rambunctious voices
Echoing through the house,
Replacing silence with Christmas glee.
Warm little bodies, hugging and laughing:
"Merry Christmas!" and "Santa was here!"
As, madcap, they dash to the tree
And finally to the windows
To see the snow lit up by the sun,
Awe in their pink-cheeked faces,
Love swelling my heart for my children
And the Son who was born this day.

Strawbery Banke Museum in Portsmouth, New Hampshire.
Photograph © Jerry & Marcy Monkman/DanitaDelimont.com

At Christmastime

William D. Hicks

Mirrored silver balls are placed
precisely on fragrant boughs
as cotton-candy-colored lights
bubble blue throughout the night.

Tossed tinsel drapes
high limbs and low branchlets
near the upper-floor steps
where the tree-stand sits.

Beneath, a knitted green skirt
blankets the floor
where a baby Jesus rests
in a brown cradle-nest.

In the corner
white-dressed packages
trimmed with ringlet bows
line a wall far away from the kitten's twitchy nose.

A star above shines
on a river of wishes
that flows past towers in this city of gifts
to end at the sea of childhood bliss.

Christmas Morning

Elsie Melchert Fowler

This is the magic morning—
Tumble out of bed,
Tiptoe down the long stairs
Softly on each tread.
Oh, what's this before you?
Rub your sleepy eyes—
Golden lights and silver,
Beautiful surprise!
Sparkling tree of wonder,
Gifts, enchanting, new—
Magic, magic morning,
Christmas dream come true!

OPERATION CHRISTMAS BLESSING

Michelle Medlock Adams

She was the sweetest preschool teacher I'd ever encountered, and my girls absolutely adored her. She was June Cleaver and Carol Brady all wrapped into one happy, beautiful package, and I was very thankful that Ms. Bonnie was in my daughters' lives.

As a single mom to a preteen daughter, Ms. Bonnie managed to provide for her family, serve in the local church, volunteer at a soup kitchen, and yet always look like a million bucks. However, I had heard that she was struggling with her finances. My heart went out to her, but somehow that just didn't seem sufficient. It was time to put action behind my heartfelt sentiments.

One December Sunday, our family walked into the church foyer and noticed a large Christmas tree in the corner with little angel tags hanging on each of its branches.

"What are those?" asked Ally, my curious four-year-old.

My five-year-old, Abby, answered, "They're angels!"

"Yeah, but what's all that writing on the angels' heads?" Ally continued.

"Oh, well, that is the name of each of the angels in heaven," Abby answered, matter-of-factly.

My husband and I smiled at each other, but neither of us had the heart to correct her at that moment. We were a little late, so we grabbed the girls' hands and took our seats in the back of the sanctuary. During the service, upon explaining the meaning of the angel tree, our pastor urged each of us to take a few angel tags and purchase gifts for those children who wouldn't receive Christmas presents any other way. After the closing hymn, the girls rushed out to the angel tree and grabbed one angel tag each.

"Mom, do you think Ms. Bonnie and her daughter are on that angel tree?" Abby asked. "I don't think they'll be getting any Christmas presents either."

Abby's question took my breath away. I'd already been thinking that we should "adopt" Ms. Bonnie's family for Christmas; Abby had just confirmed that it wasn't just a good idea—it was a "God idea."

The next few weeks were filled with holiday fanfare—Christmas plays, Christmas cards, Christmas cookies, Christmas shopping, and more. In the midst of the hustle and bustle, we initiated "Operation Blessing Bonnie." We surreptitiously found out all of Ms. Bonnie's favorite things and what she might need. One of the other preschool workers helped us find out Ms. Bonnie's daughter's sizes and needs too. My girls loved being sneaky for a good cause.

As we shopped for the two angels we'd chosen from the angel tree, Ally came running up to the cart with fuzzy leopard slippers. "I know Ms. Bonnie would love these!" Ally beamed. "Can we get these, too?"

I was amazed at how excited my girls were to be shopping for others. They had quite extensive Christmas wish lists of their own. But they weren't at all concerned with their presents. Abby and Ally were totally focused on buying presents for the two angels we'd adopted and even more obsessed with making sure Ms. Bonnie and her daughter had a beautiful Christmas.

For years, I'd read the Christmas story to my daughters, explaining how God had given His very best gift to us when He sent Jesus, His Son, into the earth as a baby. They'd nod as if they understood, but I was afraid they were getting caught up in the commercialism of Christmas and forgetting the true meaning of the Christmas story. I feared they wouldn't understand the sacrifice God made for us. I worried they would grow up being takers and not givers, simply because we'd given them so much. But, at that moment, when Ally begged me to buy fuzzy slippers for Ms. Bonnie, I realized my girls were grasping the joy of giving and honoring the true spirit of Christmas. As a praying mama, that was the best gift I could've received.

As we wrapped the presents for Ms. Bonnie, her daughter, and the angels we'd adopted, we sang Christmas carols and munched on Christmas cookies. Abby made special curly bows for the top of each package, and Ally insisted we add glittery Christmas name tags. We delivered the gifts for our angels, and then we headed for the preschool. After calling ahead to make sure Ms. Bonnie was gone for the day, we placed each of her packages under her desk. Then Ally and Abby stacked her daughter's gifts in Ms. Bonnie's large cubbyhole at the front of the classroom. The girls' giggles filled the air as tears filled my eyes. I asked Abby and Ally to pray before we left. Ally kept it short and sweet: "Dear God, help this be the bestest Christmas Ms. Bonnie and her daughter ever had. Amen."

Though I don't know if it was their "bestest," I did hear from the other preschool teachers that Ms. Bonnie and her daughter had a wonderful Christmas. It was certainly our best. That year we learned that it truly is better to give than to receive. That lesson set the tone for all of our future Christmases. May this Christmas be your bestest ever!

Yuletide

Gerald A. McBreen

Remembered sounds
of not so long ago
mixed in with this year's
Christmas cheer—
Children singing, ringing bells
from door to door.
Give the gaily wrapped
package a hug of love
before you look inside.
Feel the heart's excitement,
pounding for a wish come true.
Oh, what a wonderful surprise.
It happens every
Christmastime—
our hearts, young again—
makes us happy to wrap
and tie with fancy bows
packages for youngsters
and friends.
Then, on that long-awaited
morning, sitting by the
Christmas tree,
a present on our lap,
we are as tickled as children,
wondering what great magic
awaits us inside.

All Grown Up

Garnett Ann Schultz

Perhaps you'd say I'm all grown up
And much too old for toys,
Too old to think of Santa Claus
Like little girls and boys.
And yet I love the pleasant thrill,
The happy, sweet surprise,
The packages on Christmas morn,
Those big blue wondrous eyes.

Perhaps you think that Christmas dreams
Are only for the young,
The ornaments and Christmas wreaths,
The mistletoe that's hung,
The waiting for that happy time,
The chimes on Christmas Eve,
The cookies left for Santa Claus
By those who still believe.

Perhaps you think it's just a fad,
The Christmastime parade,
For ofttimes grownups do insist
That too much fuss is made.
Why trim a tree, why wrap the gifts
In packages so bright,
Why count the days till Santa comes
That gay and wondrous night?

Perhaps you think it's not worthwhile,
And yet somehow I've found
The world takes on a special glow
When Christmas comes around.
And though 'tis true, I am too old—
In size I'm much too tall—
In heart and mind each year I find
I'm not grown up at all.

A Tale for Christmas Evening

Lucy Carruth

Now that you're tired of your toys, Sonny Boy,
And you're cocking a sleepy eye,
Climb into my lap and I'll tell you a tale
Of a time that is long gone by.

Over the sea, in a little old town—
No, your daddy was never there—
A Baby was born on the first Christmas Day,
In a place that was chill and bare.

He had no fire like the one we have here,
Where His mother would warm His toes,
Not even a roof covered over His head,
But the stars saw His eyelids close.

Yes, He was poor, but withal was a King,
As the Wise Men afar had been told;
And they came on their camels
      to bring Him rare gifts
Of frankincense, myrrh, and gold.

Where is He now? Why He's here in our home,
But don't look for Him with your eyes;
For He is the Spirit of Love, Sonny Boy,
And ev'rything good and wise.

Photograph © Jessie Walker

Christmas Song

Gail Brook Burket

How blessed were Judean hills
Whose lonely rock-strewn height
Reflected glory from the skies
Upon that holy night.

How blessed were the shepherds
Who heard the angels sing;
How blessed was the manger
Which held the promised King.

How blessed were the Magi
And the star that guided them.
And blessed are all hearts this day
Which turn toward Bethlehem.

Where Is Christmas?

Loise Pinkerton Fritz

Where is the star of Christmas,
The star the shepherds saw;
The solemnity of worship
As the Magi knelt in awe?
Where is the King born for us—
The Babe on bed of straw?

Where is the star of Christmas?
In my soul now shines the star.
The solemnity of worship?
Of my being it is part.
And where is the newborn
    Christ-Child?
Cradled in my heart.

WELCOMING THE SAVIOR

Luke 1:39–44; 2:1–7

And Mary arose in those days, and went into the hill country with haste, into a city of Juda; And entered into the house of Zacharias, and saluted Elisabeth. And it came to pass, that, when Elisabeth heard the salutation of Mary, the babe leaped in her womb; and Elisabeth was filled with the Holy Ghost: And she spake out with a loud voice, and said, Blessed art thou among women, and blessed is the fruit of thy womb. And whence is this to me, that the mother of my Lord should come to me? For, lo, as soon as the voice of thy salutation sounded in mine ears, the babe leaped in my womb for joy. . . .

And it came to pass in those days, that there went out a decree from Caesar Augustus, that all the world should be taxed. (And this taxing was first made when Cyrenius was governor of Syria.) And all went to be taxed, every one into his own city.

And Joseph also went up from Galilee, out of the city of Nazareth, into Judaea, unto the city of David, which is called Bethlehem, (because he was of the house and lineage of David:) To be taxed with Mary his espoused wife, being great with child.

And so it was, that, while they were there, the days were accomplished that she should be delivered. And she brought forth her firstborn son, and wrapped him in swaddling clothes, and laid him in a manger; because there was no room for them in the inn.

SHEPHERDS WATCHING

Luke 2:8–20

And there were in the same country shepherds abiding in the field, keeping watch over their flock by night.

And, lo, the angel of the Lord came upon them, and the glory of the Lord shone round about them: and they were sore afraid.

And the angel said unto them, Fear not: for, behold, I bring you good tidings of great joy, which shall be to all people. For unto you is born this day in the city of David a Saviour, which is Christ the Lord. And this shall be a sign unto you; Ye shall find the babe wrapped in swaddling clothes, lying in a manger. And suddenly there was with the angel a multitude of the heavenly host praising God, and saying, Glory to God in the highest, and on earth peace, good will toward men.

And it came to pass, as the angels were gone away from them into heaven, the shepherds said one to another, Let us now go even unto Bethlehem, and see this thing which is come to pass, which the Lord hath made known unto us.

And they came with haste, and found Mary and Joseph, and the babe lying in a manger. And when they had seen it, they made known abroad the saying which was told them concerning this child. And all they that heard it wondered at those things which were told them by the shepherds.

But Mary kept all these things, and pondered them in her heart.

And the shepherds returned, glorifying and praising God for all the things that they had heard and seen, as it was told unto them.

WISE MEN FROM THE EAST

Matthew 2:1–12

Now when Jesus was born in Bethlehem of Judaea in the days of Herod the king, behold, there came wise men from the east to Jerusalem, Saying, Where is he that is born King of the Jews? for we have seen his star in the east, and are come to worship him.

When Herod the king had heard these things, he was troubled, and all Jerusalem with him. And when he had gathered all the chief priests and scribes of the people together, he demanded of them where Christ should be born. And they said unto him, In Bethlehem of Judaea: for thus it is written by the prophet, And thou Bethlehem, in the land of Juda, art not the least among the princes of Juda: for out of thee shall come a Governor, that shall rule my people Israel. Then Herod, when he had privily called the wise men, enquired of them diligently what time the star appeared.

And he sent them to Bethlehem, and said, Go and search diligently for the young child; and when ye have found him, bring me word again, that I may come and worship him also. When they had heard the king, they departed; and, lo, the star, which they saw in the east, went before them, till it came and stood over where the young child was.

When they saw the star, they rejoiced with exceeding great joy.

And when they were come into the house, they saw the young child with Mary his mother, and fell down, and worshipped him: and when they had opened their treasures, they presented unto him gifts; gold, and frankincense, and myrrh. And being warned of God in a dream that they should not return to Herod, they departed into their own country another way.

The Stable Keeper
Gertie S. Howard

He made the manger sweet with hay
From fields where shepherds guarded sheep
Then, all unknowing, went away
To simple fare and restful sleep.

He stirred, half-wakened, slept again,
Once murmured "An uncommon night!"
Drawn casement lattices were vain
Against a miracle of light.

Often the mind will hear a call
The hands instinctively obey;
He knew not why he swept the stall
And bedded it with clean, fresh hay—

Till in his heart a chiming bell
Rang high and clear, and sweetly wild—
And heard excited shepherds tell
About a star, a song, a Child.

Innkeeper's Lament
Grace Noll Crowell

They told me afterward there was a light
Shone all night long above my Kahn's low roof,
Centering above the stable, radiant, white.
They tell me now it was a heavenly proof
That the Christ whom we had waited for so long
Was there—that I had turned Him from my door.
They say above the field there was a song
Such as men had never heard before.

How could I know—how could I hear or see
Other than the clamor of the crowd,
The bleating sheep, the bartering cries, the queer
And sharp demands upon me that were loud?
If they had only told me! If they had,
I would have turned the other guests away.
I believe that every one would have been glad
For the stable's shelter and a bed of hay
To give the Christ Child room. . . . Oh, surely I
Shall not be known forever as the one
Who shut his ears to a woman's needy cry,
Who closed his door upon God's holy Son!

The Little Bed

Georgia Moore Eberling

The inn was full that night,
    they said;
There was no room for a little bed.
There was a manger, full of green
Sweet hay, and it was soft and clean.

The moon shone in;
    the star was bright.
It must have been a lovely sight—
The little Baby fast asleep
There in the stall; and maybe sheep

Were lying there and sleeping too,
As all the tiny tired lambs do.
Perhaps the little donkey stood
Beside the manger, quiet and good.

Beneath the eaves
    some gray doves, maybe,
Cooed a lullabye for the Baby.
He slumbered there, the little King,
not even hearing the angels sing!

Wondering

Eileen Spinelli

Baby Jesus in the manger,
did You cry that winter night
when You saw so many faces,
strangers under starry light?

Were You cold? Or were You cozy
in those swaddling clothes You wore?
Were You startled by the wind
that blew against the stable door?

Baby Jesus, did You hear
those angel voices in the sky?
Did they soothe You, make You sleepy
as Your mother's lullaby?

CHRISTMAS NEWS

Pamela Kennedy

The message of Christmas is all about news. The Gospel writers recall how the angel Gabriel appeared to Mary, a young woman in Nazareth, announcing that she would miraculously become pregnant and bear Jesus, the Son of the Most High! A few months later, an angel gave Joseph the news that the Child carried by Mary was, indeed, conceived by the Holy Spirit. Several months after that, the birth of this holy Child was announced to an unsuspecting group of shepherds by angelic newscasters! Within hours, those same shepherds dashed around the countryside, spreading the exciting news to everyone within earshot.

Since then, people seem compelled to share the news of that first Christmas, its wonder and excitement, in story and song. Thus it was that the words and melody of "Go Tell It on the Mountain" were initially passed by word of mouth from one excited teller to the next. But this time the news was sung not by angels in the heavens nor shepherds on hillsides, but by slaves in the cotton and tobacco fields of the southern United States.

Shortly after the American Civil War, John Wesley Work, an African-American church choir director from Tennessee, recognized the value of preserving these oral musical messages. He began collecting these spirituals and encouraged his choir members not only to embrace, but also to share their unique musical heritage. When several of the young people in Work's choir enrolled at newly founded Fisk College in 1866, they became part of the Fisk Jubilee Singers, all but two of whom were newly freed slaves. By 1873 this group had completed international tours, singing before thousands, including President Ulysses S. Grant and Queen Victoria, and introducing their enthusiastic audiences to the genre of the African-American Spiritual.

It would be Work's son, John Wesley Work Jr. and his brother, Frederick Jerome Work, however, who would actually bring "Go Tell It on the Mountain" to publication in the early twentieth century in their collection, *Folk Songs of the American Negro* (1907). Building upon his father's legacy, John Wesley Work Jr. served at Fisk as a professor of Latin and Greek and led performance groups there. These choirs maintained the robust musical legacy of their forbears, passing it along to subsequent generations. In songs and spirituals preserved by John Wesley Work Jr. and later by his son, John Wesley Work III (1901–1967), the Negro folk song would eventually be recognized and archived as a distinct musical form.

In his writings, John Wesley Work III, a gifted and prolific composer, recalls fond childhood memories of growing up on the Fisk campus and hearing the strains of "Go Tell It on the Mountain" sung by college students at daybreak each Christmas morning. It is his arrangement of this favorite carol that popularized it throughout the world, and continues to spread the good news of Christ's birth "over the hills and everywhere!"

Go Tell It on the Mountain

Traditional Words and Music

Go tell it on the moun-tain, o-ver the hills and ev-'ry-where;

Fine

Go tell it on the moun-tain that Je-sus Christ is born.

1. When I was a seek-er, I sought both night and day; I
2. He made me a watch-man up-on the ci-ty wall, and
3. Down in a low-ly man-ger, the hum-ble Christ was born; and

D.C.

asked the Lord to help me, and He showed me the way.
if I am a Christ-ian, I am the least of all.
God sent out sal-va-tion that bless-ed Christ-mas morn.

THE MEANING OF CHRISTMAS

Fulton J. Sheen

Wise men came from the East, perhaps Persia. They saw the Babe—a Babe whose tiny hands were not quite long enough to touch the huge heads of the cattle, and yet hands that were steering the reins that keep the sun, moon, and stars in their orbits. Shepherds came, and they saw a Baby's lips that did not speak, and yet lips that might have articulated the secret of every living man that hour. They saw a Baby's brow under which was a mind and intelligence compared with which the combined intelligences of Europe and America amount to naught.

One silent night, out over the white-chalked hills of Bethlehem, came a gentle cry. The great ones of the earth did not hear it, for they could not understand how an Infant could be greater than a man. At the Christ Child's birth, only two groups of people heard that cry: the shepherds, who knew they did not know anything; and the Wise Men, who knew they did not know everything. Let us reach out at this holy Christmas season to accept Christ with humility and love.

Festive barn in Colorado. Photograph © 2011 Alaskastock/Masterfile Corporation

THE PONDERING HEART

J. Harold Gwynne

At the time of Jesus' birth, the little town of Bethlehem was crowded with visitors and filled with confusion and excitement. It was like a great homecoming for those who belonged to the house and family of King David. The matter of their lodging being cared for, the visitors could give themselves over to the pleasures and opportunities of the occasion. They could meet and mingle with old friends and acquaintances, spend the time of their brief sojourn in discussing the news of the day, and recall memories of past good times together. It was a glad, gay, busy and carefree occasion, such as most holidays afford.

Only a few immediate relatives and close friends paid any attention to the distress of Mary and Joseph. When Mary's Child was born, the news quickly spread throughout the village. The women all knew it first and told their husbands; but the busy crowds of visitors gave it little thought. "Did you hear that a poor peasant woman from Nazareth gave birth to a son last night?" "Yes, and what a pity she had to go through such an ordeal at this time and in such a place!" "Why, they say that she had to dress the baby with her own hands, and lay him in a manger!" An interesting item of news, a bit unusual to be sure, but for most of the visitors, just a means of passing the day. When they went back to their homes after completing the business of enrollment, they remained in complete ignorance of the meaning of the event that had come to pass in Bethlehem while they were there. Although it was the greatest event of all time, those who were closest to it knew nothing of its meaning.

There were a few, however, who gained impressions that remained with them all of their lives. Some shepherds came in from nearby fields with a wonderful story to tell. They found Mary and Joseph and the Baby, lying in the manger, and related what the angel had said to them concerning this Child. "And the shepherds returned, glorifying and praising God for all the things that they had heard and seen, as it was told unto them" (Luke 2:20). Of course, they never forgot the experience of that wonderful night when the angels of heaven spoke good tidings to them and sang their hymn of glory and of peace.

The shepherds repeated again and again the saying of the angel. The people who heard their story were filled with wonder and astonishment. "But Mary kept all these things, and pondered them in her heart" (Luke 2:19). She was neither surprised nor astonished as were the inhabitants of Bethlehem. She and Joseph had both been prepared for these miraculous events by the revelations of the angels. Mary did not tell her experiences at this time but kept them quietly in her heart.

Photograph © IngridHS/Shutterstock Images

We may be assured that the Christmas treasures we keep will belong to the heart and the spirit. In Mary's experience, the angels went away again into heaven; the shepherds withdrew and went back to their sheepfolds; the Wise Men presented their costly gifts and departed. The swiftly moving scenes of new lands and peoples passed before her eyes, but the wonderful revelations concerning the Savior were treasured in her heart forever. It is a very strange thing that, as far as we know, Jesus never returned to Bethlehem, the scene of His birth. But we may be sure that Mary made many a pilgrimage in memory to the place where she laid her firstborn Son in the lowly manger.

The way of the pondering heart is our road to Bethlehem. We may go there in our thoughts as we meditate upon the story of Christmas. Like the shepherds of old, we must resolve to make this pilgrimage. It requires an act of will and determination on our part. "Let us now go even unto Bethlehem" (Luke 2:15). Many will not go; they will be too busy with the outward paraphernalia of Christmas. But we must determine to go; we must go now, before it is too late. It is not an easy matter to go; we must take time; we must make sacrifices; we must put aside pressing matters. But we must go, even though the way be difficult, if we are to find the Christ and the new life He has for us.

THE CHRISTMAS HEART

George Matthew Adams

*T*he Christmas heart is a beautiful heart—for it is full of love and thoughtfulness for others. And Christmastime is a tribute to the most beautiful Heart that ever beat.

It is also the time in which we are reminded of our own inadequacies and helplessness of spirit. For during this season, we are so bathed in Yuletide-inspired unselfishness that we feel our failures and lacks as never before in the entire year. It is well this way, for we may therefore resolve anew to live better and stronger lives for those who mean so much to us.

So let us cherish this Christmas heart and keep it all through the year to come.

Let us turn on all the lights in this heart, so that it will be aglow to the world; and let us push up the shades of the windows in this heart, so that everyone who passes may be cheered and inspired.

Let us remember that the Christmas heart is a giving heart, a wide-open heart that thinks of others first.

The birth of the Baby Jesus stands as the most significant event in all history because it has meant the pouring of healing love into a sick world, a love that has transformed all manner of hearts for more than two thousand years and given to human service the beauty it would never have had otherwise.

Underneath all the bulging bundles of the season is this beating Christmas heart. Wrapped around even the tiniest gift is this same loveliness of thought and heartfelt expression.

What a happy New Year it would be for all if we would carry this same Christmas heart into every day during the coming year and make it a permanent thing in our lives.

*Photograph © toriru/
Shutterstock Images*

Season's Greetings

Virginia Blanck Moore

I find no fresh and different ways
To wish you happy holidays;
no novel phrase that can convey
my heartfelt hope your Christmas Day
will bring you peace and happiness;
no newfound wording to express
my hope the season's wonted cheer
will last you through the whole new year.

But though my words may not be new,
the message still rings fresh and true
each time I wish you season's cheer
with "Merry Christmas!" . . . "Glad New Year!"

ISBN-13: 978-0-8249-1338-0

Published by Ideals Publications
A Guideposts Company
Nashville, Tennessee
www.idealsbooks.com

Publisher, Peggy Schaefer
Editor, Melinda L. R. Rumbaugh
Copy Editor, Debra Wright
Designer, Marisa Jackson
Permissions Editor, Patsy Jay

Cover: *Christmas Village* by Richard Burns. Copyright © 2011 by Richard Burns/Applejack Art Partners
Inside front cover: Painting by George Hinke. Image from Ideals Publications
Inside back cover: Painting by Donald Mills. Image from Ideals Publications
Art for "Bits & Pieces" by Kathy Rusynyk; texture page 28 © Dioscoro L. Dioticio/Shutterstock Images; texture pages 38–39 © dinadesign/Shutterstock Images.
"Go Tell It on the Mountain" sheet music by Dick Torrans, Melode, Inc.

Readers are invited to submit original poetry and prose for possible use in future publications. Please send no more than four typed submissions to: Magazine Submissions, Ideals Publications, 2630 Elm Hill Pike, Suite 100, Nashville, Tennessee 37214. Manuscripts will be returned if a self-addressed stamped envelope is included.

ACKNOWLEDGMENTS:

ARNOLD, EMMY. "Christmas Joy" from *When the Time Was Fulfilled*, 1965, published by Plough. Reprinted in *Watch for the Light*, by Orbis Books and in *Plough*'s 2001 edition. Used by permission Plough Publishing House. ARTLEY, BOB. "Christmas Trees Remembered" from the *Annual of Christmas Literature and Art Volume 60* copyright © 1990 Augsburg Fortress Publishers. Reproduced by permission. All rights reserved. BAUER, FRED. "Time for Christmas" from *The Guideposts Christmas Treasury*. Copyright © 1972 by The Guideposts Association. Used by permission of Shirley Bauer. CARRUTH, LUCY. "A Tale for Christmas Evening." From *The Christian Herald*, 1951. CHUTE, MARCHETTE. "One Night" from *Rhymes About the Country*. Copyright © 1941, The Macmillan Company. CROWELL, GRACE NOLL. "Innkeeper's Lament," used by permission of Claire Cumberworth, and "This Would I Keep" from *The Christian Herald*, 1951. FISHER, AILEEN. "Christmas Shoppers" from *Year-Round Programs for Young Players*. Copyright © 1985 Aileen Fisher. Used by permission of Marian Reiner on behalf of the Boulder Public Library Foundation, Inc. FROST, FRANCES MARY. "Christmas in the Woods" from *Christmas Bells are Ringing*. Copyright © 1942 by Harper Collins Publishers. MAUL, DEREK. "Christmas Eve: A Little Light for the New Year" from *In My Heart I Carry a Star: Stories for Advent*. Copyright © 2008 by The Upper Room. Used by permission of the author. MCQUILLEN, LOUISA GODISSART. "Touch the World" from *When Seasons Change*. Copyright © 2000. Used by permission of the author. SHAW, LUCI N. Quote from "Circled with Light," *Wintersong*. Used by permission of Regent College Publishing. SHEEN, FULTON J. "The Meaning of Christmas" from the writings of Fulton J. Sheen. Used by permission of The Society for the Propagation of the Faith. OUR THANKS to the following authors or their heirs for permission granted or for material submitted for publication: George Matthew Adams, Georgia B. Adams, Michelle Medlock Adams, Deborah A. Bennett, Virginia Blanck, Nancy A. Brackett, Gail Brook Burket, Georgia Moore Eberling, Nancy Esher, James Feig, Elsie Melchert Fowler, Loise Pinkerton Fritz, J. Harold Gwynne, William D. Hicks, Elizabeth A. Hobsek, Frank H. Keith, Pamela Kennedy, Gerald McBreen, Nanci Roth Natale, Anne Penrod, Alice Kennelly Roberts, Garnett Ann Schultz, and Eileen Spinelli. GUIDEPOSTS NEW YORK: "The Secret of Happy Giving" by Catherine Marshall. Copyright © 1974 and "Grammy's Crèche" by Elaine St. Johns from *Guideposts Family Christmas*. Copyright © 1980 by Guideposts. All rights reserved.

Every effort has been made to establish ownership and use of each selection in this book. If contacted, the publisher will be pleased to rectify any inadvertent errors or omissions in subsequent editions.